Tour de Courage

HOW MY FIRST TRICYCLE RIDE CHANGE EVERYTHING

To My Mom:

Who let me do something very hard

by myself, and in so doing, helped

me for the rest of my life.

Special thanks to Connie Krygowski for painting the pictures in this book, which were drawn by Michael Bortolotto.

Michael & Dorothy Bortolotto
Nanaimo, British Columbia, Canada
www.positiverebel.com.com

ISBN-13: 978-1516828487

Other books by Michael Bortolotto:

"The Truth About Apples & Pineapples:It's What's Inside That Counts"
A Cure For Bullying
Copyright ©The Positive Rebel 2011

Printed in Nanaimo, BC
Published by:

Communication Ink Media & Public Relations
25 Cavan Street
Nanaimo, BC V9R 2T9
www.communicationink.ca

Forward

Michael Bortolotto's moving tale of his learning to overcome the challenges of riding his tricycle as a toddler is not a book for children alone. Rather it is an insight into parenting, teaching, coaching, and any other life experience where we are called upon to raise children.

My daughter found the book sad and a little uncomfortable at times, as she worried Michael's mother would not rescue him from his difficulty right away. However, as we read on and talked about it further, we realized that what his mother was doing was what good parents do: allowing him to grow as independently as was safe for a boy his age. Always loving, watching for his well being, celebrating his achievement in a way that respected his needs for autonomy in growing, his mother endured the toughest experience of disciplined parenting. She stood by as he tried and failed, knowing that he would only succeed in life and find sense of self if he did.

Within this is a lesson for the classroom, the hockey rink, the soccer field, homework time, the dinner table and all the places where we observe our child's exploration for growth. Places where as vicarious adults, our needs for control, feelings of success through our child's experience, and own self-worth can flourish unchecked. Caring from afar, unavoidably living and dying inside every scrape and tumble, but practicing the hardest of parenting behaviours, non-interference is a magical, yet not always comfortable, clear example of what love looks like.

As a manager of adults in the workplace, the book is also an excellent reminder for me of the needs of my staff young and old to be respected as they find their way in their jobs. To stand by and allow them to feel safe in their temporary failures and not rescue them requires both faith and patience. Once again, the difficult task of practicing non-interference is in reality, the meeting of the most important needs of the people I work with: confidence of autonomy, self-worth and sense of purpose.

I always enjoy and value hearing Michael speak, or reading what he writes. He simply gets it. I encourage others to do the same.

Brian Nikula, MA Ed
Principal
Springwood Middle School
Parksville BC

"Hey!!! What are doing?!?
Please put my son down!!!
Michael will ride that tricycle by himself!!"

That loud voice was coming from my Mom,
as she ran down the driveway towards
both of us, waving her arms and
hands above her head.

The neighbour, who had rushed to my rescue
after watching me fall off my tricycle
several times, and hearing me crying
in pain, quickly sat me back down on
the paved street, took her hands away
from me, and stood back.

I remember that as my Mom ran towards me,
I thought to myself, "Is she finally coming to
help me ride my tricycle?"

To my surprise, Mom ran right past me to
where the neighbor was, and explained to her,
"Please don't help him. I know
he can ride the tricycle by himself!"

Mom then quickly turned, crouched down,
put her hand on my shoulder, and said,
"Michael, I know you can ride your
tricycle on your own." Then she smiled,
stood up, and began walking up
the driveway to our house.

Shortly after disappearing through the
front door, she reappeared and stood
in the front living room window.
I started crying again, but she remained
where she had been standing when all my
troubles of riding my new tricycle began.

If this sounds confusing, let me explain. I was
only four years old, and trying to learn how to ride
my new, red and white tricycle for the very first time.
It was very difficult for me. Because I have Cerebral
Palsy, I have poor body coordination, awful balance,
and unexpected muscle spasms. Riding a tricycle
was a challenge for me, and at the same time,
an experience that would change my life.

It was early afternoon on a sunny, spring day when my Mom decided it was time for me to ride my new tricycle. Before venturing out onto the street, she dressed me in a cute pair of blue, short pants, a blue short-sleeved t-shirt, and black running shoes.

Once my running shoes were tied, she picked up
the tricycle and said, "Come on Michael,
it's time for you to learn to ride your tricycle."
Together we headed out the front
door and walked toward
the quiet, paved street.

Due to having trouble working my legs, poor
balance, and the small, crushed gravelly rock
on the driveway, I had to walk slowly so
I wouldn't fall down and hurt myself.

Halfway to the street, my Mom passed me,
going back to our house. As she went by,
I stopped her and asked, "Where are you going?
Aren't you going to help me ride the tricycle?"
She pointed towards the street and said, "Michael,
go ride your tricycle." So, I continued on my
way to where she had left it.

While slowly walking to the street, I thought,
"Oh, boy! I'm finally going to get to ride
my new toy I received for Christmas!"
This made my muscles begin to twitch,
shake, and tremble with excitement.
My first challenge was to calm down
and stop the twitching, shaking and
trembling motions in my legs, arms,
hands and fingers.

Once all my muscles were calm,
I reached for the tricycle's handlebars
with both hands, and put my right foot
on the bottom step. I thought to myself,
"Wow! This is going to be a lot of fun!"

As I began to lift my left foot up off the pavement, the tricycle suddenly started rolling forward on the street by itself! This made me feel scared. I panicked, lost my balance, and fell, crashing onto the pavement, scraping my knee.

The pain of scraping my left knee and the
sight of blood dripping from it, made me cry
and yell really loudly for Mom. While crying
and looking at her through my teary eyes,
I realized my mom wasn't coming out
to the street to help me!

Instead, she just stood in the front window,
making a circling motion with both her
arms to encourage me to ride the tricycle.
I thought to myself, "What is happening?
Why isn't she coming out to help
and comfort me?"

After getting over the feeling of being scared
of the tricycle and my Mom's reaction,
I slowly stood back on my feet and stared
at the tricycle like it was a big, red and white
monster with rubber tires that wanted to hurt me.

With both of my hands shaking, I put them on
the handlebars, and raised my right foot onto
the bottom step of the tricycle. I carefully
lifted my left foot off the ground, until it
was also on the bottom step of the tricycle.

With all my courage, I inched myself up towards
the white seat and then disaster struck again!
I lost my balance, and WHAM! I hit the ground.
This time I was bleeding from a large cut
on my right elbow.

Through each teardrop in my eyes, I searched
to see if my Mom was coming to help and
comfort me. When I spotted her in the front
window, all she did was make circling motions
with both arms. She wanted me to keep
trying to ride my tricycle.

Like a good little foot soldier, I struggled back onto my feet for a third time. Just like before, my efforts ended in a hard crunch, and this time I was sitting next to the tricycle, bleeding from a scrape on my chin.

As I lay there beside my tricycle, afraid, I peaked at the front window, and sure enough, there was my Mom, standing there motioning with both arms, waving in a circle, encouraging me to keep trying to ride the tricycle. I thought to myself, "Why won't she come and help me?"

Just like before, I picked myself up and began to climb towards the seat of the tricycle. That's when something different happened. During the process of raising my left foot towards the bottom step of the tricycle, I felt two warm, strong hands grab me around the waist and lift me onto the seat.

Quickly, I flung my head back to see who was
helping me. It was the lady from the house next door!
She had come to rescue me from the big, red
and white, steel monster with rubber tires!

Just as my little behind was about to touch
the top of the tricycle's white seat, we both
heard a loud voice coming towards us.
"Hey!!! What are you doing?!?
Please put my son down!!
Michael will ride that
tricycle by himself!!"

It was my Mom, racing down the driveway,
asking the neighbour to stop
and please put me down!

The neighbour put me back down on the paved
street, stepped back, and spoke to my Mom for a
couple of minutes. After they finished talking,
they both went back into their houses, and I was
left sitting next to the tricycle, by myself, crying.

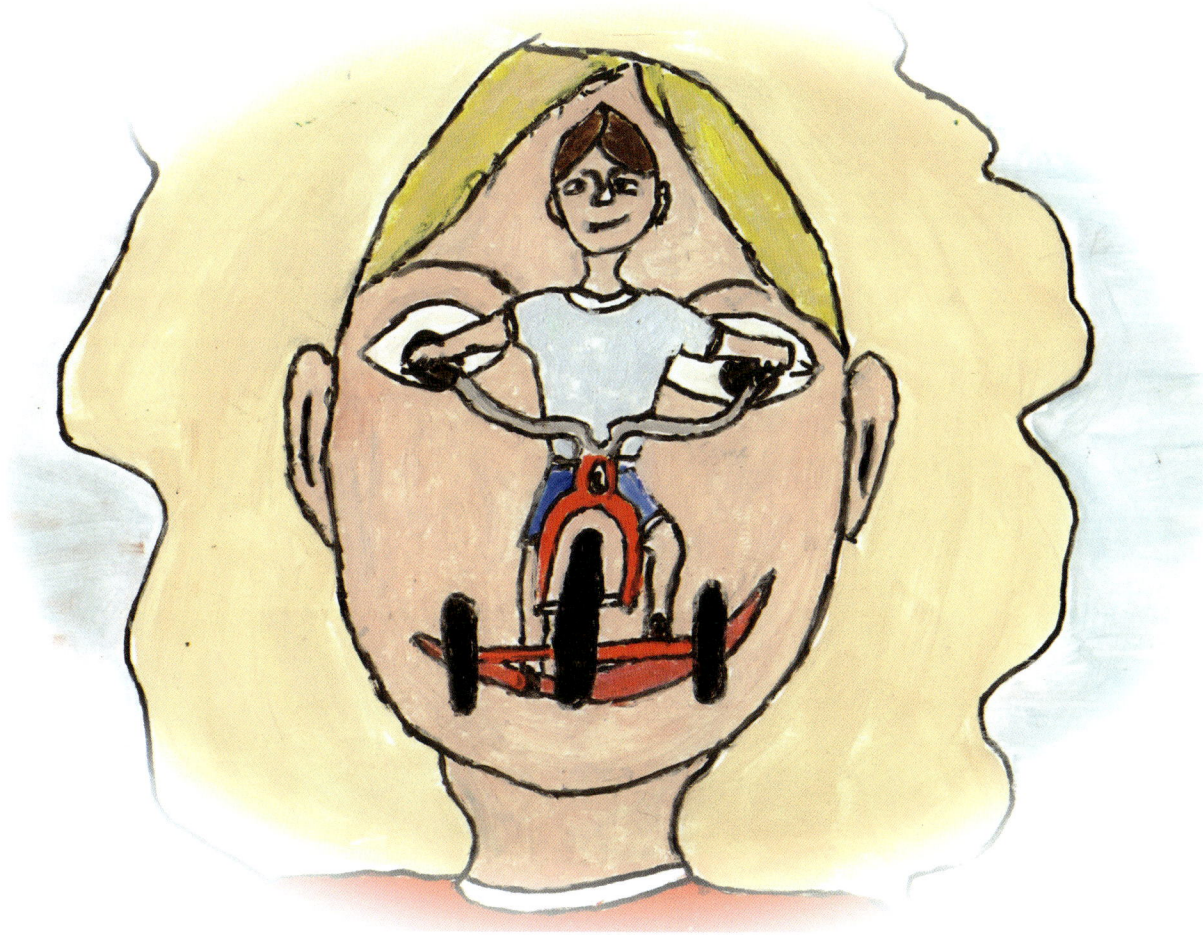

While sitting there, a strange thought went through my
mind, causing me to change from being scared
and alone, to courageous, determined and persistent.
I then jumped up and put both hands on the handlebars
and my feet on the bottom step of the tricycle.

Taking a deep and determined breath, I pulled
myself onto the white seat and put my feet
on both peddles. Hanging on for dear life,
my legs started pushing the pedals, and the
tricycle began moving along the street.
Finally, I was riding it!!
It was an amazing feeling!

Many years later, Mom and I were sitting alone
on the couch after Thanksgiving dinner. Mom looked
at me and said, "Michael, we both have a lot to be
thankful for. We have a nice home, a good family,
and plenty of good memories."

I quickly disagreed, reminding her of the time
she had left me alone as I was trying to learn
how to ride my new, shiny, red tricycle. I asked
her why she didn't come and help me when
I was crying and bleeding from the scrapes
on my knee, elbow and chin.

With tears in her eyes, she said, "Michael,
you didn't see the whole picture. . . .While you were
falling off the tricycle, I was standing
behind the curtains, crying!"
Although it was very hard for her to stay
in the house, my Mom knew if she went
out to the street, she'd be helping me
for the rest of my life.

Mom wanted me to learn how to be courageous and use
determination, perseverance and the power of
positive thought to overcome limiting challenges
and what seemed to be impossible obstacles
that she knew I'd face in my life.

This made me stop and think:
despite having Cerebral Palsy, my courage,
determination, perseverance and positive thoughts have
allowed me to ride a tricycle and a mountain bike;
drive a car and a fire truck; graduate from
high school and college; be a husband and
father, and how to break through the limiting
challenges and what seems to be impossible
obstacles created within my mind.

So the next time you are faced with a
limiting challenge or what seems to be an impossible
obstacle that is causing fear and doubt in your mind,
start thinking positively. Be brave and act right now!
And of course, never give up!

Printed in Great Britain
by Amazon